Live Free

DISCOVERY SERIES BIBLE STUDY

For individuals or groups

The search for freedom is a universal pursuit. From teenagers testing their parents' standards to employees wondering how closely they are being monitored by the boss, we all wonder where the barriers stop and the independence starts. Even as followers of Jesus Christ—as people who know the truth that sets us free—we yearn to live free. There's a delicious irony in all this in Galatians 5:22–23, a passage that spells out what is called the "fruit of the Spirit." Author Constantine R. Campbell calls the Spirit's guidance "evidence that God is gradually . . . taking control of more and more of our lives." Yet this is also true: Allowing the Holy Spirit's fruit to manifest itself is a source of deep, abiding freedom for all of us. Join us as Campbell helps us walk through this vital passage, which can help us truly *Live Free*.

Dave Branon
Our Daily Bread Ministries

This Discovery Series Bible Study is based on
Live Free (Q0214), one of the popular Discovery Series booklets from Our Daily Bread
Ministries. Find out more about Discovery Series at
discoveryseries.org

Discovery House is affiliated with Our Daily Bread Ministries,
Grand Rapids, Michigan.

Requests for permission to quote from this book should be directed to:
Permissions Department, Discovery House, PO Box 3566, Grand Rapids, MI 49501,
or contact us by e-mail at permissionsdept@dhp.org

Discovery House.
from Our Daily Bread Ministries

Managing Editor: Dave Branon
Study Guide questions: Dave Branon
Graphic Design: Steve Gier

COVER PHOTO:
Daniel Wanke via Pixabay.com

INSIDE PHOTOS:
Michał Lech via Pixabay.com, p.6; Andreas N. via Pixabay.com, p.12; Creative Commons, p.14;
Mconnors via MorgueFile.com, p.15; Ronnieb via MorgueFile.com, p.20; Nokta_cizgi via Pixabay.com, p.22;
Earl53 via MorgueFile.com, p.23; Public Domain via Pixabay.com, p.28; Teetasse via Pixabay.com, p.30;
Davidperrot34 via Pixabay.com, p.31; Colette Tessier via Pixabay.com, p.34; PDPics via Pixabay.com, p.36;
Hilde Stockmann via Pixabay.com, p.37; Patryk Specjal via FreeImages.com, p.42; Gojo23 via MorgueFile.com, p.44

ISBN: 978-1-62707-539-8
Printed in the United States of America
First Printing in 2016

Table of Contents

How To Use
DISCOVERY SERIES BIBLE STUDIES

The Purpose

The Discovery Series Bible Study (DSBS) series provides assistance to pastors and lay leaders in guiding and teaching fellow Christians with lessons adapted from Discovery Series booklets from Our Daily Bread Ministries and supplemented with items taken from the pages of *Our Daily Bread*. The DSBS series uses the inductive study method to help Christians understand the Bible more clearly.

The Format

READ: Each DSBS book is divided into a series of lessons. For each lesson, you will read a few pages that will give you insight into one aspect of the overall study. Included in some studies will be FOCAL POINT and TIME OUT FOR THEOLOGY segments to help you think through the material. These can be used as discussion starters for group sessions.

RESPOND: At the end of the reading is a two-page STUDY GUIDE to help participants respond to and reflect on the subject. If you are the leader of a group study, ask each member to preview the STUDY GUIDE before the group gets together. Don't feel that you have to work your way through each question in the STUDY GUIDE; let the interest level of the participants dictate the flow of the discussion. The questions are designed for either group or individual study. Here are the parts of that guide:

MEMORY VERSE: A short Scripture passage that focuses your thinking on the biblical truth at hand and can be used for memorization. You might suggest memorization as a part of each meeting.

WARMING UP: A general interest question that can foster discussion (group) or contemplation (individual).

THINKING THROUGH: Questions that will help a group or a student interact with the reading. These questions help drive home the critical concepts of the book.

DIGGING IN: An inductive study of a related passage of Scripture, reminding the group or the student of the importance of Scripture as the final authority.

GOING FURTHER: A two-part wrap-up of the response: REFER suggests ways to compare the ideas of the lesson with teachings in other parts of the Bible. REFLECT challenges the group or the learner to apply the teaching in real life.

OUR DAILY BREAD: After each STUDY GUIDE session will be an *Our Daily Bread* article that relates to the topic. You can use this for further reflection or for an introduction to a time of prayer.

Go to the Leader's and User's Guide on page 45 for further suggestions about using this Discovery Series Bible Study.

THE Spirit's Fruit

Harvest season is a time of reward.

The countless hours of work, the perspiration, the constant watering, the diligent guarding against threats, and even the dirt under the fingernails all become worthwhile when our gardens, orchards, and vineyards produce their crops.

The life cycle of plants in our gardens ensures satisfying and delicious results. But growth in our Christian lives is rarely as dependable and never as predictable as the fruit on the trees or the vegetables in our gardens. Despite the agonizing work and the hours spent trying to cultivate maturity, we often perceive only minor results—or failure.

Paul's imagery of the fruit of the Spirit describes Christian maturity with a clarity and vividness that makes us want to harvest those sweet, juicy fruits. But why does it always seem just out of reach? No matter how hard we try, we never seem to attain the patience we expect or the peace we so desperately desire. Perhaps a fresh look at the fruit of the Spirit will help us understand who is responsible for growing it—and how that helps us in our pursuit of Christlikeness.

> If the Holy Spirit is producing the fruit of the Spirit in your life, you are Spirit-filled.
>
> HERB VANDER LUGT

Whose Fruit Is It?

Some years ago when my children were younger, I took them to a concert featuring Australia's favorite kids' entertainer and country music star, Colin Buchanan. When we were waiting to get in, I overheard one mother encouraging her complaining young son, "Now remember, Johnny, patience is a fruit of the Spirit."

I remember thinking how strange that sounded. I was so used to hearing, "patience is a virtue," that "patience is a fruit of the Spirit" somehow seemed the wrong thing to say. The more I thought about that phrase, the more uneasy I felt. Not with the woman's statement—which of course is true—but with my reaction. I was starting to feel challenged, since her words seemed to reflect a more godly way of thinking than mine.

While there is nothing wrong with virtue, it is not the same thing as fruit of the Spirit. Anyone can have virtue or many virtuous qualities. They are usually self-cultivated. A "virtuous person" is someone who has disciplined herself to be patient or brave or generous. On the other hand, "fruit of the Spirit" implies something quite different. Most obvious perhaps is that it's the Spirit's fruit, not ours. No amount of determination or discipline ripens the fruit of the Spirit. And because it is the Spirit's fruit, it is a harvest that only those who have the Spirit of God in them can have.

Standing there with my kids, I wondered why it had never occurred to me to say, "patience is a fruit of the Spirit" when trying to calm them down. In the past I had probably asked them to be patient or to be self-controlled, but I wasn't thinking in spiritual terms. So I was reminded of something that day: I needed to let the words of Scripture influence my parenting.

I'm grateful for that brief moment of encouragement. But the more I've thought about it, the more I've wondered whether it's right to "apply" the fruit of the Spirit like this. Of course it's appropriate to encourage our kids in godly attitudes and behaviors. And it's good to remind them of what the Bible says.

> "To set the mind on the flesh is death, but to set the mind on the Spirit is life and peace."
> ROMANS 8:6 (ESV)

Of course our kids should know that Scripture guides our attitudes and behaviors. So what exactly is the problem with encouraging someone by saying "patience is a fruit of the Spirit"?

The problem becomes a little clearer when we realize that when Paul listed the fruit of the Spirit in Galatians 5:22–23, he did not intend it to be a set of instructions. It actually serves an entirely different purpose but still has implications for the way we live.

> "The fruit of the Spirit is a gift of God,
> and only He can produce it."
>
> DIETRICH BONHOEFFER

In order to get the idea of what Paul is saying, it may help to imagine a target. By starting small with Galatians 5 (the bull's-eye) and moving out to the bigger rings—how the fruit of the Spirit connects to the message and purpose of the whole letter of Galatians, and the significance of the fruit of the Spirit in the unfolding plan of God revealed in the Bible—we can better understand what Paul is saying about the fruit of the Spirit. My hope and prayer is that the Spirit would encourage our hearts as we stop to wonder at the awesome love of God in Christ and the power of the Spirit in our lives. Let's look now at Galatians 5.

"Fruit of the Spirit" and "acts of the flesh"

When we read about the fruit of the Spirit, we often zoom in tightly on just two verses. While these are great verses, if we focus on them exclusively we can get a distorted picture of their meaning and significance. We need to read about the fruit of the Spirit listed in Galatians 5:22–23 in its setting. That is the bull's-eye.

The *fruit of the Spirit* is set in contrast to the *acts of the flesh*, listed immediately before in 5:19–21.

> *The acts of the flesh are obvious: sexual immorality, impurity and
> debauchery; idolatry and witchcraft; hatred, discord, jealousy, fits of
> rage, selfish ambition, dissensions, factions and envy; drunkenness,*

orgies, and the like. I warn you, as I did before, that those who live like this will not inherit the kingdom of God.

*But the fruit of the Spirit is love, joy, peace, forbearance, kindness, goodness, faithfulness, gentleness and self-control. Against **such things** there is no law (emphasis added).*

Those lists of attitudes and traits couldn't be more different. They are almost polar opposites. But placing negatives and positives side by side like this is a common writing technique—one that Paul, the writer of Galatians, uses from time to time (EPHESIANS 4:25–32). Listing negatives and positives next to each other sharpens their meanings. White looks brightest against a black backdrop. The fruit of the Spirit stands in sharp contrast against the works of the flesh. The difference is night and day.

As we compare these lists and imagine people characterized by these traits, it becomes obvious that the second list is the better of the two. Those are the characteristics we want. But the contrast between the individual traits is not the most significant difference between these two lists. At the heart of the contrast are the different sources of the characteristics.

> Let's live and walk in the Spirit so that the fruit of joy will naturally burst forth.
>
> JOANIE YODER

The first is a list of acts of the *flesh.* The list is a set of outcomes of the *power* of the flesh. The flesh is the driving force and origin of those characteristics. When the flesh is at work, this is the result. The flesh is good at what it does; its works are *obvious,* Paul says. If anyone is familiar at all with Picasso, it's easy to spot his work. It is so distinct that it's tough to mistake it for someone else's work. So too the acts of the flesh are easily recognizable.

Likewise, the fruit of the Spirit is produced by the Spirit. Fruit grows out of something—a tree or a vine—and the growth of the fruit is entirely powered by its host. Take a budding apple off the branch of an apple tree, and it will not grow any further. The tree is the essential source of nutrients for the apple. So too the fruit of the Spirit is entirely dependent upon its source—the Holy Spirit himself. Just as the *acts* in verses 19 through 21 come from the flesh, the *fruit* is grown by the Spirit.

The Spirit's Fruit

MEMORY VERSE
Galatians 5:16—

"Walk in the Spirit, and you will not gratify the desires of the flesh."

To begin to understand the usefulness of Paul's image of fruit in describing the Spirit's role in the harvest of good qualities.

Warming Up

How are the "acts of the flesh" being manifested in today's society?

Thinking Through

1. What does Con Campbell mean when he says on page 8: "It's the Spirit's fruit, not ours"? How does that begin to help our thinking about Galatians 5:22–23?

2. Is it a little surprising to read Campbell's assertion that Paul "did not intend [the fruit of the Spirit] to be a set of instructions"? Explain your reactions to this statement.

3. What sets up this teaching so clearly is the contrast between the "acts of the flesh" (vv. 19–21) and the "fruit of the Spirit" (vv. 22–23). According to the author, why did Paul put these so close together?

Going Further

Refer

These verses speak of the contrast between sinful acts and what the Holy Spirit produces.

Romans 8:5: What effect does Spirit control vs. flesh control have on the mind?

Romans 7:5: If they are not controlled by salvation and the Holy Spirit, what do the sinful passions of the flesh lead to?

1. Think for a moment about Paul's words, "the acts of the flesh are obvious" (v. 19). What does the fact that sinful acts are "obvious" tell us about our sin nature and mankind's propensity to disobey God?

¹⁹ The acts of the flesh are obvious: sexual immorality, impurity and debauchery; ²⁰ idolatry and witchcraft; hatred, discord, jealousy, fits of rage, selfish ambition, dissensions, factions and ²¹ envy; drunkenness, orgies, and the like. I warn you, as I did before, that those who live like this will not inherit the kingdom of God.

2. That is quite a list Paul compiled. Notice that it includes some items that most followers of Christ would never do and some that are a part of many believers' lives. Do Christians sometimes split sins into *acceptable* and *unacceptable* categories? Is this right?

3. Paul's final words in this short passage are chilling. What does he mean about people who "live like this"? Are their actions condemning them or has their rejection of Jesus left them vulnerable to these things? Or something else?

Prayer Time

Use the *Our Daily Bread* article on the next page as a guide for reflection on the fruit of the Spirit.

Reflect

1. If I find any of the acts of the flesh listed in Galatians 5:19–21 present in my life, what steps do I need to take to get them out?

Precious Fruit

How much would you be willing to pay for a piece of fruit? In Japan, someone paid more than $6,000 for one Densuke watermelon. Grown only on the northern Japanese island of Hokkaido, this beautiful dark-green sphere looks like a bowling ball. The nearly 18-pound watermelon was one of only a few thousand available that year. The fruit's rarity allowed it to bring an astronomical price on the market.

Christians have fruit that is far more precious than the Densuke watermelon. It's called the fruit of the Spirit: "love, joy, peace, forbearance, kindness, goodness, faithfulness, gentleness and self-control" (GALATIANS 5:22–23). Each "fruit" is a different aspect of Christlikeness. In the Gospels, we see how Christ exemplified these virtues. Now He wants to produce them in our hearts—in what we say, how we think, and how we respond to life (JOHN 15:1–4).

A rare and delicious fruit may bring a premium price in the marketplace, but Christlike character is of far greater worth. As we confess all known sin and yield to God's indwelling Spirit, our lives will be transformed to the likeness of Christ (1 JOHN 1:9; EPHESIANS 5:18). This spiritual fruit will fill our lives with joy, bless those around us, and last into eternity.

—*Dennis Fisher*

GALATIANS 5:22–23 —

The fruit of the Spirit is love, joy, peace, forbearance, kindness, goodness, faithfulness, gentleness and self-control.

■ Read today's *Our Daily Bread* at **odb.org**

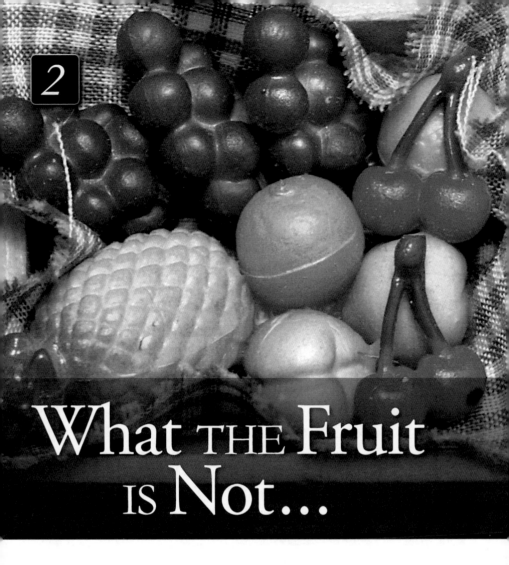

2

What THE Fruit IS Not...

The first important thing to understand about the fruit of the Spirit is that it is the fruit of the *Spirit*. These famous verses have strong implications for the way we live, but whose fruit is it? They are the Spirit's. We must understand that these characteristics are produced by the third person of the Trinity. He is the agent, the source, and the power that grows the fruit. And His power is contrasted to that of the flesh; they are two competing sources of our actions and attitudes.

The fruit of the Spirit is indicative, not imperative.

Indicative and *imperative* are ten-dollar words that simply mean the difference between an observation of the way things are (indicative) and a command or instruction to do something (imperative). Considering the previous point (that it's the Spirit's fruit), this makes sense. The significance of this shouldn't be overlooked. This means that the fruit of the Spirit is not a to-do list. These verses do have implications for how we live (and we'll get to that), but Paul does not say, "live like this, like this, and like that" before he lists the fruit of the Spirit. Fruit grows from the Spirit. It's not the result of our hard work or discipline, and it's not a list to check off when we feel we've "got it down." It's not even a list to put on our wall to remind ourselves of things we need to work on. It's not a list of imperatives—commands for us to follow. It's a list of indicatives—it's just the way things are.

If Galatians 5:22–23 were a list of demands, it would sound something like this:

You must love each other, have joy, be at peace with God and each other, and be patient with one another. You have to be kind and good and have faith; you need to be gentle and exercise self-control.

Let's be honest. That may not be how we read those verses, but that is how many of us understand and apply them. But that's not what the text says, is it? The list is indicative rather than imperative; it tells us what is. Paul writes, "The fruit of the Spirit is..." This is simply the way things are. Where the Spirit is, these fruit grow.

Now don't misunderstand. Not all believers will necessarily exhibit all these characteristics. Even though Christians have the Spirit of God living in them, it doesn't mean that everyone who has the Spirit will always be loving, joyful, patient, and so forth. What I mean is that these things are the fruit of the Spirit; they flow from Him, and He produces them. So when they are present in a follower of Christ, it is evidence that the Spirit is in them. The Holy Spirit may choose to grow the fruit of peace in my life, joy and patience in you, and faithfulness and love in your neighbor. They are His fruits to grow as He sees fit—for the benefit of the believer, the church, and God's kingdom.

The list is not exhaustive.

Another reason we shouldn't use Galatians 5:22–23 as a to-do list is that this may not be an exhaustive list of the fruit of the Spirit, and it would be a mistake to pursue these traits to the exclusion of some other character qualities. This may be a new idea to some. Let's take a few moments to explore this possibility.

Look again at the negative list: the works of the flesh in 5:19–21. That certainly does not seem like an exhaustive list, does it? Admittedly, it covers a lot. But it doesn't include murder. Doesn't it seem that murder could be described as a work of the flesh? And that is just one thing that isn't listed. There are many more. By the same token, I'm sure many more positive qualities could rightly be called fruit of the Spirit—traits such as generosity, hospitality, and humility, just to mention a few.

■ **FOCAL POINT**

Notice these suggestions for **letting the Spirit guide us**: Galatians 5:16: "walk by the Spirit"; v. 18 "led by the Spirit"; v. 25 "live by the Spirit"; v. 25 "keep in step with the Spirit."

It's easy to puzzle over lists like this and wonder, *If there were more, why didn't Paul include them? Why not mention generosity, hospitality, and humility?* I think that kind of question leads to a dead end. It's not the point; and if we spend too much time thinking about it, we lose sight of the point that is being made. Lists like this are not intended to be exhaustive, and we shouldn't read too much into the things they might omit. Rather, "vice and virtue" lists are intended to provide a sketch of common characteristics. They give the idea through broad brushstrokes. We get the gist of the works of the flesh and the fruit of the Spirit from these lists; we don't get an exhaustive description.

Will all believers have all the fruit in equal measure?

It's common to assume that the list of the Spirit's fruit indicates what *every* Christian is supposed to look like, in equal measure. Or to put it another way, we might not expect the Spirit-filled believer to be lacking in, say, kindness or self-control. If the same Spirit is in all believers, then surely He will produce the same fruit in each one, right?

But is that assumption correct? This passage is *descriptive*. It sketches out some of the fruit the Spirit produces in the lives of believers. But some believers might be more joyful than others; some will be gentler than others; some

■ FOCAL POINT

Look at the various references to the Holy Spirit in Galatians 5. First, there is the promise of future righteousness that we await "through the Spirit" (v. 5). Next, there is the challenge to "walk by the Spirit" (v. 16). Paul then lists what is "contrary to the Spirit" (vv. 17–21). Following that are the "fruit of the Spirit" (vv. 22–23). And finally he concludes with this great reminder: "Since we live by the Spirit, let us keep in step with the Spirit" (v. 25).

will have greater self-control than others. In this way, the fruit of the Spirit could be understood in parallel to the *gifts* of the Spirit.

We could think the same way about the fruit of the Spirit. He is the same Spirit in each of us, yet He will produce different fruit in us in different ways. This means that someone who is hospitable and generous but who perhaps lacks a little in the joy department can display the fruit of the Spirit just as much as someone who knows joy but lacks hospitality. Of course, in an ideal world, we would all display all the fruit of the Spirit in equal measure—to the max!—but that's just not the way it is.

Perhaps the fruit of the Spirit, like the gifts of the Spirit, are to be thought about in more corporate terms. While no one *person* will have *all* the gifts of the Spirit, the church as a whole certainly will. Maybe we should think that way about the fruit of the Spirit. I'm sure most, if not all, congregations exhibit all the fruit of the Spirit collectively. Perhaps this is what Paul was implying. He was, after all, writing to the church in Galatia. Far too often we read the Bible overly individualistically, in this case leading us to think that each individual ought to show all the fruit of the Spirit. But Paul may have been thinking in more corporate terms. He may have been sketching a picture of a gathering of believers who together exhibit the characteristics listed in Galatians 5:22–23.

What the Fruit Is Not…

To begin to understand how to think about the fruit of the Spirit.

MEMORY VERSE
Galatians 5:18—

"If you are led by the Spirit, you are not under the law."

Warming Up

What do you know about the way the Holy Spirit interacts in the lives of Christians? What are His roles in your life?

Thinking Through

1. Con Campbell says, "The fruit of the Spirit is not a to-do list" (p. 16). So what do you see as the difference between being "led by the Spirit" (v. 18) and being told not to follow a "to-do" list?

2. Two words Campbell uses to try to explain how the fruit of the Spirit is to interact with our lives are *indicative* and *imperative*. What does each mean in relation to the fruit of the Spirit?

3. As Campbell points out on pages 18 and 19, not all Christians demonstrate all of the fruit of the Spirit the same way. What do you think of the "corporate" view at the end of page 19?

Going Further

Refer

Fruit has other sources in our lives besides from the Holy Spirit. See what sources each of these verses give for fruit.

Philippians 1:11

Colossians 1:6

James 3:17

1. This passage speaks of fruit that comes from being connected to the Savior—the "true vine." Like the "indicative" fruit of Galatians 5:22–23, this fruit comes to us through Jesus—not through our actions. In this case (vine-fruit), what must we do, according to verses four and five?

2. This passage suggests an all-or-nothing perspective about fruit. What can we do apart from the vine? What does it mean to "remain in" Jesus (v. 4)?

3. There seems to be a difference in approach between John 15 and Galatians 5. John 15:5 says that if we remain in Jesus we will _____. In Galatians 5:25 we are to keep _____ with the Spirit. What is the difference?

[1] "I am the true vine, and my Father is the gardener. [2] He cuts off every branch in me that bears no fruit, while every branch that does bear fruit he prunes so that it will be even more fruitful. [3] You are already clean because of the word I have spoken to you. [4] Remain in me, as I also remain in you. No branch can bear fruit by itself; it must remain in the vine. Neither can you bear fruit unless you remain in me.

[5] "I am the vine; you are the branches. If you remain in me and I in you, you will bear much fruit; apart from me you can do nothing. [6] If you do not remain in me, you are like a branch that is thrown away and withers; such branches are picked up, thrown into the fire and burned. [7] If you remain in me and my words remain in you, ask whatever you wish, and it will be done for you. [8] This is to my Father's glory, that you bear much fruit, showing yourselves to be my disciples.

Prayer Time ▶

Use the *Our Daily Bread* article on the next page as a guide for reflection on the fruit of the Spirit

Reflect

1. John 15 doesn't say what fruit we will bear as we abide in Jesus. What do you think the difference is between the fruit spoken of here and the specific fruit of Galatians 5?

2. How can we make sure we "remain in" Jesus?

Turkish Delight Syndrome

I n C. S. Lewis's classic *The Lion, the Witch and the Wardrobe*, Edmund was easily won over to the side of darkness by the wicked white witch. Her method was simple—she appealed to his love for rich, sweet food, as well as for status and revenge. The Turkish Delight she offered him was delicious, and it left him craving even more. So strong was its appeal that it led him to betray his brother and sisters.

The appetites of the world and the flesh are powerful and addictive tools of the devil. He appeals to our love for what satisfies our selfish and sinful desires and uses it to tempt, control, discourage, defeat, and destroy us. We crave power or money or food or alcohol or clothes or sex, even though we are in danger of sacrificing our friends, our loved ones, and even our relationship with our Savior to satisfy our desires.

How can we resist the temptations of Satan? Paul said, "Walk by the Spirit, and you shall not gratify the desires of the flesh" (GALATIANS 5:16). He also wrote, "Clothe yourselves with the Lord Jesus Christ, and do not think about how to gratify the desires of the flesh" (ROMANS 13:14). And John said, "Do not love the world or anything in the world" (1 JOHN 2:15).

Put on the Lord and walk in the Spirit. That's how to break the power of the Turkish Delight syndrome.

—*David Egner*

ROMANS 13:14—

Clothe yourselves with the Lord Jesus Christ, and do not think about how to gratify the desires of the flesh.

■ Read today's *Our Daily Bread* at **odb.org**

What THE Fruit IS...

We've spent the last few moments considering what the fruit of the Spirit is *not*. Now it's time to consider what it *is*. The simplest description of the fruit listed in Galatians 5:22–23 is that they are *characteristics*. Notice that they are not abilities (though many of the gifts of the Spirit involve abilities). They are not *doing* words. They are *being* words. Someone is gentle; someone is loving; someone is self-controlled. Yet, while this is true, *being* always leads to *doing*. This is one way the fruit of the Spirit intersects with how we act.

If someone is gentle, it will be evident by gentle conduct and manner. If someone is loving, it will be expressed in acts of love. If someone is self-controlled, it will be demonstrated in self-control. Perhaps that's a subtle distinction, but it's an important one. Being leads to doing. The Spirit isn't interested in just changing certain behaviors—adding some and removing others; He is interested in *changing who we are as people*. Changed people do changed things. But the internal change has to come first. God doesn't want us to be robots who always do the right thing but whose character is, well, robotic. God is after our *hearts*.

Something that is easy to overlook is the fact that most of the fruit mentioned is relational. Love, peace, patience, kindness, goodness, faithfulness, and gentleness are all about relating to others. What is love, if not extended toward others? I might say that *I love jazz*, which obviously is not a person. But that's not the kind of love in view here. This love is relational, between two or more persons.

Peace is not about being in a peaceful Zen state in which nothing fazes us. The biblical notion of peace, or *shalom*, is a state of good relations between two or more parties.

Patience and kindness are obviously relational. Patience is primarily relational in that it has to do with tolerant forebearance of others. Kindness has to do with caring for others and looking out for their needs.

■ A WORD ABOUT JOY

The Bible doesn't say joy is a fruit of circumstance; it clearly states that joy is a fruit of the Spirit (GALATIANS 5:22). To live a joy-filled life, we must "walk in the Spirit" (V. 25). Then we can rejoice in spite of our circumstances. Paul was in prison when he said, "Rejoice in the Lord always. I will say it again: Rejoice!" (PHILIPPIANS 4:4).

—JOANIE YODER

> These are the virtues our Lord wants us to cultivate. These are the virtues that are at the same time gifts of God. God promises to reward these traits in us, not because they flow from our own intrinsic righteousness, but because, as Augustine put it, "God is pleased to crown His own gifts."
>
> R. C. SPROUL

While goodness may be less clearly relational, true goodness is demonstrated in relationships. We might think of ourselves as a "good person," but if we are always mean-spirited or angry toward others, our "goodness" is rather thin.

Faithfulness is always relational. It involves loyalty and commitment to someone. In the Bible, faithfulness is never abstract, like being obedient to a list of rules. Instead, faithfulness is always about our relationship with God. If we are faithful to Him, we will follow His commands. But just obeying the rules is not the point; obedience is an expression of faithfulness.

Gentleness is relational. Our interaction with other people demonstrates our gentleness. We might think of ourselves as "gentle" because we're pacifists and wouldn't hurt a fly and are always careful with delicate things. But if we treat people harshly, our gentleness is not a fruit of the Spirit.

The only two characteristics that are not obviously relational are joy and self-control. These seem to be more inward in the sense that they are not necessarily expressed in relation to other people. We can have joy without anyone else around. We can show self-control in private. But even these characteristics have relational applications. Our joy can be shared with others. And self-control often involves respecting the dignity of others and not infringing on their well-being.

The fruit of the Spirit has significant implications for our relationships with each other. This is a core emphasis of the godly life in Christ Jesus; we all need to get along with each other by showing love, patience, and kindness in all our interactions.

So, what do we do about this?

I've been making the case that Galatians 5:22–23 is not a to-do list. It's indicative, not imperative. But surely there are implications for the way we live, right? Well, certainly. First we need to understand how the fruit of the Spirit fits in the big picture of the Christian life.

Immediately after the list, Paul says, "Those who belong to Christ Jesus have crucified the flesh with its passions and desires" (GALATIANS 5:24). This verse relates to the "vice list" of 5:19–21. Notice that Paul does *not* say: "Don't do these things." Instead, he appeals to the deeper way of thinking. He appeals to a spiritual reality. If we belong to Christ Jesus, we have *crucified the flesh*. Now, remember that the vice list is introduced as the *acts of the flesh*. Flesh is the power that produces such practices.

But in 5:24 Paul says that the flesh has been crucified. It has been put to death with Christ. Because we belong to Christ Jesus, we are united with Him in His death. Spiritually, we have been put to death. We are no longer subject to the power of the flesh. This is so much more than a simple command to

> Because we belong to Christ Jesus, we are united with Him in His death. Spiritually, we have been put to death. We are no longer subject to the power of the flesh. This is so much more than a simple command to avoid certain behaviors.

avoid certain behaviors. A radical change has taken place, and we no longer belong to the realm of the flesh, enslaved by its passions and desires. We now belong to the realm of the Spirit.

In the following verse, Paul says, "Since we live by the Spirit, let us keep in step with the Spirit" (5:25). We live by the Spirit. We no longer live by the flesh; the Spirit is the power in the Christian life. We are under His authority and control. And if we live by the Spirit, then we are to *follow the Spirit.* To follow the Spirit, or to keep in step with the Spirit, means that we live in a way that is consistent with Him. We learn what the Spirit wants us to be like, and we seek to be like that. We align our will with the will of the Holy Spirit. We get in sync with Him. Ultimately, that means we will desire to be marked by the fruit of the Spirit. We will want to be loving, joyful, peaceful, kind, good, faithful, gentle, and self-controlled.

But how is that different from treating the fruit of the Spirit as a to-do list? I've already argued that it's a list of indicatives, not imperatives, and that's certainly true. But the imperative comes in verse 25: We are to follow or keep in step with the Spirit. That's different from treating the fruit as imperatives, because our wills are to be aligned with the third person of the Trinity. We are to cooperate with Him. If we do, He will produce His fruit in us. If we do not, we will remain immature believers who look more fleshly than spiritual.

This means that the Spirit does not simply zap us to become the mature, godly believers He desires us to be. I suppose He could do that if He chose, but generally God chooses not to work like a microwave, but more like a slow-cook oven. As the Spirit slowly "cooks" us, it is our job to stay in the oven, as it were. We can't cook ourselves, but we can allow God to do the cooking.

To understand more deeply what it means to keep in step with the Spirit, we need to think a little more broadly about Galatians as a whole. We turn to this next.

3

To grasp the meaning of the words that are described as the fruit of the Spirit.

MEMORY VERSE
Galatians 5:22–23 —

"The fruit of the Spirit is love, joy, peace, forbearance, kindness, goodness, faithfulness, gentleness and self-control."

Warming Up

What five characteristics would people use to describe you? How closely do those terms mirror the fruit of the Spirit?

Thinking Through

1. On page 23 Con Campbell points out that the words used to describe the fruit of the Spirit are *characteristics*—and they are *being* words. As you think about how God wants to change us on the inside, how does Campbell's two-pronged definition help you understand what God wants from us?

2. Campbell goes on to say that most of the words are *relational*. How does that reality work into how God wants us to live?

3. Toward the end of this section, Campbell says we are to "follow the Spirit." What does that mean, and what does it have to do with the fruit of the Spirit?

Going Further

Refer

It might a good idea to do a little word study of each of the fruit of the Spirit. Why not start with *gentleness*. Examine its meaning and use in these verses:
Philippians 4:5
Colossians 3:12
1 Timothy 6:11
1 Peter 3:15

1. *Joy* is one of the words used in this passage that is less relational and more individual. What kind of joy comes to a believer who is walking in step with the Spirit? How, then, does that joy spill out to others in a relational way?

> [22] But the fruit of the Spirit is love, joy, peace, forbearance, kindness, goodness, faithfulness, [23] gentleness and self-control. Against such things there is no law.

2. As you look at the relational aspect of love, peace, patience, kindness, goodness, faithfulness, and gentleness, discuss how each of those can help a believer influence those outside of faith.

3. The introduction on page 1 speaks of freedom. Here we see Paul saying, after mentioning the fruit of the Spirit: "Against such things there is no law." How does the Spirit's fruit give you that kind of freedom?

Prayer Time ➤

Use the *Our Daily Bread* article on the next page as a guide for reflection on the fruit of the Spirit.

Reflect

How can following the Spirit in a way that enhances these nine characteristics help you get along with others and be the kind of shining light for Jesus He wants you to be?

Can't Take It Back

I **couldn't take my actions back.** A woman had parked her car and blocked my way of getting to the gas pump. She hopped out to drop off some recycling items, and I didn't feel like waiting, so I honked my horn at her. Irritated, I put my car in reverse and drove around another way. I immediately felt bad about being impatient and unwilling to wait thirty seconds (at the most) for her to move. I apologized to God. Yes, she should have parked in the designated area, but I could have spread kindness and patience instead of harshness. Unfortunately it was too late to apologize to her—she was gone.

Many of the Proverbs challenge us to think about how to respond when people get in the way of our plans. There's the one that says, "Fools show their annoyance at once" (PROVERBS 12:16). And "It is to one's honor to avoid strife, but every fool is quick to quarrel" (20:3). Then there's this one that goes straight to the heart: "Fools give full vent to their rage, but the wise bring calm in the end" (29:11).

Growing in patience and kindness seems pretty difficult sometimes. But the apostle Paul says it is the work of God, the "fruit of the Spirit" (GALATIANS 5:22–23). As we cooperate with Him and depend on Him, He produces that fruit in us. Please change us, Lord.

—*Anne Cetas*

GALATIANS
5:22–23
The fruit of
the Spirit is . . .
gentleness and
self-control.

■ Read today's
Our Daily Bread at
odb.org

THE
Bible's Orchard

Paul wrote the letter to the Galatians because the Christians there had started to believe a different gospel. They had begun to think that Gentile (anyone who was not Jewish) Christians must follow Jewish customs in order to be truly Christian. Paul wrote to remind them that faith alone in Jesus Christ, not works of the law, saved them.

Paul introduces the Spirit in chapter 3 by asking if the Galatians received the Spirit by obeying the laws of Moses or by believing what they heard about Jesus.

He reminds them that Jesus redeemed them so they might be blessed by receiving the Spirit. God adopted them and sent the Spirit into their hearts as a sign of that adoption. As sons and daughters, they are free, not slaves. And since they are free, they shouldn't turn around and make themselves slaves again.

But, Paul warns, this new freedom that comes from our adoption by God and the coming of the Spirit should not be used to indulge our own selfish desires. Instead, the newfound freedom should be used to serve each other in love. Walking by the Spirit would help the Galatians not to gratify the desires of the flesh. The works of the flesh and the fruit of the Spirit are both obvious. It is easy to tell if actions are selfish or motivated by the Spirit. Since the flesh no longer controls them, they should live by the Spirit.

This brief synopsis of Galatians shows how the Spirit fits into Paul's explanation of the Christian life, and therefore how we should think about the fruit of the Spirit. The Spirit is the sign of adoption into God's family—He is the sign of freedom. Living by the Spirit is the answer to the problem Paul set out to address. Do Gentile Christians need to live by Jewish customs? No! Followers of Jesus should live according to the Spirit.

Galatians and the Old Testament

What Galatians says about God and life for those who follow Christ intersects with some of the biggest themes of the Bible. The promises to Abraham (SEE GENESIS 12:1–3) are fulfilled in Christ, since people of all nations are blessed through faith in Him. The justice demanded by the law of Moses is satisfied in Christ's crucifixion. In the book of Galatians, life under the law is contrasted to the new life under the Spirit. This new life is the result of a promise given long ago. The promise that the Spirit of God would dwell within His people is first given by the Old Testament prophet Ezekiel.

The promise in Ezekiel 36:27 is especially interesting for understanding the fruit of the Spirit in Galatians 5. In that passage the Lord says, "I will put my Spirit in you and move you to follow my decrees and be careful to keep my laws." We've already seen from Galatians that the presence of the Spirit is the sign of new life. Because of Christ's death on the cross that paid the penalty for sin and our redemption through faith in Him, the presence of the Spirit in Christians' hearts fulfills the first half of Ezekiel 36:27. But it's the second half of the verse that connects most directly to the fruit of the Spirit. The Lord says He will put His Spirit within you and move you to follow His decrees and laws. In other words, the Spirit of God will enable the people of God to live His way.

The second half of Ezekiel 36:27 is fulfulled in the fruit of the Spirit. The Spirit brings forth love, joy, peace, forbearance, kindness, goodness, faithfulness, gentleness, and self-control in the lives of believers. And notice what Paul adds at the end of Galatians 5:23: "Against such things there is no law." The point here is that if the Spirit is growing His fruit in your life, you will be living in line with the law of God. Christians are not bound by the law of Moses, but their lives will nonetheless live up to the moral standards set in the law. But this doesn't happen through "law-keeping" or being good; rather, it will happen by keeping in step with the Spirit.

The fruit of the Spirit is part of the grand plan of God to enable His people to live in a way that pleases Him—living by the power of the Spirit. As members of God's family—adopted sons and daughters—God shapes us to be like Him and to bear the characteristics that flow from His own character. The fruit of the Spirit is nothing less than the culmination of centuries of promise and expectation that finds fulfillment as the result of Jesus's life, death, and resurrection. What a privilege to be Spirit-filled people!

The Bible's Orchard

To begin to understand the role of the Holy Spirit in God's grand design.

MEMORY VERSE

Ezekiel 36:27—

"I will put my Spirit in you and move you to follow my decrees and be careful to keep my laws."

Warming Up

In what ways have you realized or recognized the blessing of having the Holy Spirit in your life?

Thinking Through

1. Notice that Con Campbell points out an important prophecy about the Holy Spirit in Ezekiel 36:27: "The promise that the Spirit of God would dwell within His people." What does it mean to you to see that this is an Old Testament promise?

2. Think about the idea that the presence of the Holy Spirit guides us to live "in line with the law of God," as Campbell puts it on page 33. How does that guidance indwelling our being—our heart—tie in with our freedom from the law? In other words, why is it more advantageous to have an internal guide than an external guide?

3. Think about Campbell's statement that "God shapes us . . . to bear the characteristics that flow from His own character" (p. 33). What might some of those characteristics be?

Going Further

Refer

The presence of the Holy Spirit can be found throughout the Old Testament. What do we find out about the work of the Spirit in these passages?

Genesis 1:2   Exodus 31:3   Job 32:8   Job 33:4   Psalm 143:10   Nehem. 9:20

1. Look at Ezekiel 36:26. What an amazing picture of the transformation that takes place when a person trusts Jesus as Savior! What are some of the results of having our "heart of stone" replaced with a "new heart"?

> 26 I will give you a new heart and put a new spirit in you; I will remove from you your heart of stone and give you a heart of flesh. 27 And I will put my Spirit in you and move you to follow my decrees and be careful to keep my laws.

Galatians 5:24–25

> 24 Those who belong to Christ Jesus have crucified the flesh with its passions and desires. 25 Since we live by the Spirit, let us keep in step with the Spirit.

2. When Ezekiel says God's Spirit moves us to "follow [God's] decrees," what practical help does that give us in our lives?

3. Though the Spirit works in our lives, we are not to remain passive. What does it mean to "keep in step with the Spirit"?

Prayer Time ▶

Use the *Our Daily Bread* article on the next page as a guide for reflection on the fruit of the Spirit.

Reflect

1. What does it say about God's grand design that the coming of the Spirit into our lives was predicted by Ezekiel more than 500 years before the incarnation of Jesus?

2. Does having a better knowledge of the idea of keeping step with the Spirit take a little pressure off in regard to living by rules and regulations? In what way?

Fragrant Fruit

We were privileged to be the guests of some friends who live in the mountains. When we entered our room, we were pleased to find a lovely basket of fresh fruit on the table. The grapes, pears, apples, and strawberries looked refreshing and delicious. But it was not until we cut or bit into the fruit that we experienced the full aroma and flavor.

Paul likened the characteristics of the Holy Spirit's work in our lives to fruit (GALATIANS 5:22–25). The delectable arrangement he described includes love, joy, peace, and kindness. Like the fruit in our guestroom, the full "flavor" is best released under cutting or trying circumstances.

Love, for example, is most beautiful when encountered by hatred. Peace is most welcomed when it blossoms in the midst of conflict. Forbearance and self-control are sweetest in the face of bitter persecution and temptation.

One reason God allows us to experience trials is that through our godly response the true value of the fruit of the Spirit is released as a witness to the world.

The next time we are tested, may our deepest desire be to allow the Holy Spirit to produce in us fragrant fruit for the glory of God.

—*David Egner*

1 PETER 2:21—

Christ suffered for you, leaving you an example.

■ Read today's
Our Daily Bread at
odb.org

Keeping IN Step WITH THE Spirit

We've explored what the fruit of the Spirit is (and what it isn't) and why it matters. We turn now to consider how the fruit of the Spirit shapes Christian living.

It is wonderful to consider all that God has done for us in Christ and continues to do through the Holy Spirit. For all He has done, our responsibility is simple: Keep in step with the Spirit and resist the flesh. We are to cooperate with the work He is doing as we look forward to the day when the power of the flesh will be conquered.

One of the most important things the Spirit does is to point us to Christ. That means one way we can keep in step with the Spirit is to fix our eyes on Jesus. Let our daily thoughts and meditations return to Him time and time again. Let Him be the center of our thoughts, our imagination, and our desires. As we choose to follow Christ, to depend on Him, and to submit to Him, we will be keeping in step with the Spirit.

As we reflect on Jesus, we have opportunity to express our dependence on Him for all things, not the least of which is our salvation. He is the source of eternal life, and indeed of all life as the ruler and sustainer of the entire cosmos. Our prayerful dependence on Christ brings Him honor and is the right disposition of our hearts. All such reflection on Christ and expression of our dependence on Him is produced through the influence of the Spirit.

But we all know too well the reality that the Christian life is a struggle. While the Spirit does indeed work powerfully within us, the Scriptures exhort us to resist living according to the flesh. This assumes that we can still give ourselves over to the power of the flesh. We are not given the option of being passive. So throughout the Christian life, there is an ongoing tension between living by the Spirit and giving in to our own selfish desires.

A good daily prayer is to ask God for the strength to remain engaged in the struggle. There are only two ways the struggle can stop feeling like a struggle. The first is to die and be with the Lord. The second is to give up the struggle and give in to the flesh. This is the option we must avoid! So we need to be on our guard against feelings of hopelessness that discourage us to remain in the fight.

Though it will sometimes feel like it, our battle against the flesh is not hopeless. There are two major reasons for this: We are no longer under the authority of sin, and the Spirit is a deposit guaranteeing our future inheritance. Let's explore these in turn.

We are no longer under the authority of sin. Paul develops this point in greatest detail in Romans 6. If we have died with Christ, we have been set free from sin (ROMANS 6:7). What Paul means by "sin" in Romans 6 is sin as a *power*, or ruler. The point he is making is that, by dying with Christ, believers have been released from sin's power; we now live under Christ's authority. Yet Paul appeals to the Romans not to put themselves under sin again (6:12–13). While sin is no longer our master (6:14), the pull to go on "obeying" sin is real and powerful. But Paul wants us to realize that we don't have to give in.

Our struggle with sin is real. Sin once ruled over us, and our bodies were conditioned to obey its demands. It's the way we lived our entire lives until we were set free by Christ. Now that we know spiritual freedom, our comprehension of it can take a while to catch up. Occasionally, sin calls out, "Come here!" and our initial impulse is to obey. But in Christ we are no longer slaves to sin. We do not need to obey its call. Yet we will feel its pull and even struggle with our first reaction to give in to its demands. Even though we are free, we can choose to do what it says, even though sin has no right to tell us what to do.

> A good daily prayer is to ask God for the strength to remain engaged in the struggle.

So, we live this life with an ongoing tension between the Spirit and our former rulers: sin and the flesh. We are to go on choosing the Spirit. We belong to Christ now, and His Spirit is powerful. Let us keep in step with the Spirit, and deny the illegitimate call of the conquered powers of sin and the flesh.

The second major reason our battle against the flesh is not hopeless is that it will one day come to an end. As Paul says in Ephesians 1:13–14, the Spirit is a seal marking the fact that we belong to Christ. And He is a deposit guaranteeing our inheritance, until He finally redeems us. This means that the Spirit is the proof of our future. The presence of the Spirit is the sign of the new age, and we know that Spirit-filled people will one day be fully transformed with new resurrection bodies, and we will be, once and for all, totally free from sinning.

Paul puts this in a similar way in Romans 8:14–17. Those who are led by the Spirit of God are the children of God, since He is the Spirit of adoption. In fact, the Spirit enables us to cry "*Abba*, Father," and testifies that we are God's children. The punch line comes in verse 17, "If we are children [of God], then we are heirs—heirs of God and co-heirs with Christ." While we suffer with Him, we will also be glorified with Him. So we see that the presence of the Spirit in our lives points forward to a glorious future—a future without sin, suffering, or shame as the glorified children of God.

The tension between the flesh

The fruit of the Spirit is not a to-do list to check off. The Spirit produces the fruit in us. Christianity is not a set of rules, nor is the Bible a manual for good living. Christianity is about a relationship with God the Father, through His Son Jesus Christ, empowered by the Holy Spirit.

and the Spirit goes on until that day. But as we continue to live according to the Spirit, as we strive to keep in step with Him, and as we resist the call of the flesh, the Spirit will continue to produce His fruit in us.

Harvest Time

The fruit of the Spirit is love, joy, peace, forbearance, kindness, goodness, faithfulness, gentleness, self-control, as well as other Christlike characteristics. The Spirit lives in us because new life has come in Christ, and we have been set free from slavery to the flesh, sin, and the law. He is the sign of the new

■ A WORD ABOUT PEACE

The world we live in cannot offer peace. It offers only poor options. Pleasure, power, and possessions are no substitute for peace of heart and mind.

Paul reminded the believers at Philippi, "The peace of God, which transcends all understanding, will guard your hearts and your minds in Christ Jesus" (PHILIPPIANS 4:7). This is the peace God brings to those who have been reconciled to God by faith in His Son Jesus (EPHESIANS 2:14–16). It is a peace we are to share with a world that is desperate for it.

Peace—real peace—is found only in a relationship with Jesus. Have you received His peace?

—BILL CROWDER

age and is the seal of our membership in God's family. The Spirit works in us to produce fruit that is in keeping with the family likeness as we fix our eyes on Jesus, remain fully dependent upon Him, and seek to worship Him in all of life.

The fruit of the Spirit is not a to-do list to check off. The Spirit produces the fruit in us. Christianity is not a set of rules, nor is the Bible a manual for good living. Christianity is about a relationship with God the Father, through His Son Jesus Christ, empowered by the Holy Spirit.

5 Keeping in Step with the Spirit

STUDY GUIDE
read pages 37–41

To examine how the fruit of the Spirit shapes Christian living.

MEMORY VERSE
ROMANS 8:1–2 —

"There is now no condemnation for those who are in Christ Jesus, because through Christ Jesus the law of the Spirit . . . has set you free."

Warming Up

Can you recall the circumstances when the Holy Spirit pointed you to Jesus for salvation? How did the Spirit move your spirit to want to trust Jesus as Savior?

Thinking Through

1. Con Campbell writes about allowing Christ to be our focus as a key component of keeping in step with the Spirit. What practical things can we do to keep our focus on Jesus throughout the day?

2. One of the most debilitating battles a Christian faces is the ongoing influence of sin. How does Romans 6:5–7 help us with that battle?

3. We may grow weary in the battle, but Ephesians 1:13–14 has the ultimate promise of relief for us. What role does the Holy Spirit play in the future time when we will be "fully transformed with new resurrection bodies" (p. 40)?

Going Further

Refer

Notice what the Holy Spirit offers in these verses:
Romans 14:17
1 Thessalonians 1:6
2 Timothy 1:14
Titus 3:5
Hebrews 2:4

1. What an amazing promise we find in Romans 8:2! How would you put in your own words what the Holy Spirit gives us in that verse?

2. What does it mean in practical terms that we "do not live according to the flesh but according to the Spirit" (v. 4)?

3. In this world where chaos seems to reign, we can find great solace and hope in Romans 8:6. As we seek to live out the fruit of the Spirit from Galatians 5:22–23, what additional help and comfort do we find in Romans 8:6 regarding the Holy Spirit?

[1] Therefore, there is now no condemnation for those who are in Christ Jesus, [2] because through Christ Jesus the law of the Spirit who gives life has set you free from the law of sin and death. [3] For what the law was powerless to do because it was weakened by the flesh, God did by sending his own Son in the likeness of sinful flesh to be a sin offering. And so he condemned sin in the flesh, [4] in order that the righteous requirement of the law might be fully met in us, who do not live according to the flesh but according to the Spirit.

[5] Those who live according to the flesh have their minds set on what the flesh desires; but those who live in accordance with the Spirit have their minds set on what the Spirit desires. [6] The mind governed by the flesh is death, but the mind governed by the Spirit is life and peace.

Prayer Time ➤

Use the *Our Daily Bread* article on the next page as a guide for reflection on the fruit of the Spirit.

Reflect

Imagine a life in which we are characterized by the nine words that describe the fruit of the Spirit. What have we learned about how to appropriate those characteristics in our lives with the Spirit's help?

Walking In Step

When my daughter Ann was in the high school marching band, I loved to watch the young musicians march in step. Whether they were performing before a panel of judges at a district competition, at halftime during a football game, or on tour in Austria, they moved as one to the cadence of the drums and the lead of the drum major.

Galatians 5:25 states, "Since we live by the Spirit, let us keep in step with the Spirit." This means that as we walk along in our Christian lives, we are to follow the Spirit's lead. We are to be in harmony with Him. If we get out of step, follow a wrong cadence, or stray off the correct pathway, the results will be obvious (VV. 19–21).

How can we tell if we are walking in step with the Spirit? Paul spelled it out clearly in Galatians 5. We will not be guilty of the practices mentioned in verses 19 through 21. Rather, the fruit of the Spirit—love, joy, peace, forbearance, kindness, goodness, faithfulness, gentleness, and self-control—will be clearly evident in our lives (VV. 22–23).

How would you rate yourself when it comes to walking in step with the Spirit? Are you in cadence? Or are you following a drumbeat of your own making?

—David Egner

GALATIANS 5:25—

Since we live by the Spirit, let us keep in step with the Spirit.

■ Read today's *Our Daily Bread* at **odb.org**

● LEADER'S and USER'S GUIDE

Overview of Lessons: *Live Free*

Pulpit Sermon Series (for pastors and church leaders)

Although the Discovery Series Bible Study is primarily for personal and group study, pastors may want to use this material as the foundation for a series of messages on this important issue. The suggested topics and their corresponding texts from the Overview of Lessons above can be used as an outline for a sermon series.

DSBS User's Guide (for individuals and small groups)

Individuals—Personal Study
- Read the designated pages of the book.
- Carefully consider the study questions, and write out answers for each.

Small Groups—Bible-Study Discussion
- To maximize the value of the time spent together, each member should do the lesson work prior to the group meeting.
- Recommended discussion time: 45 minutes.
- Engage the group in a discussion of the questions—seeking full participation from each member.

Note To The Reader

The publisher invites you to share your
response to the message of this book
by writing Discovery House,
P.O. Box 3566, Grand Rapids, MI 49501,
USA. For information about other
Discovery House books, music,
or DVDs, contact us at the same address
or call 1–800–653–8333. Find us online at
dhp.org or send e-mail to **books@dhp.org**.